Healthy Kids

Sleeping Well

Sylvia Goulding

CHERRYTREE
BOOKS

Published in 2006 by The Evans Publishing Group
2A Portman Mansions
Chiltern Steet
London W1U 6NR

Printed in China

British Library Cataloguing in Publication Data

Goulding, Sylvia
   Healthy eating. - (Healthy kids)
   1.Nutrition - Juvenile literature
   I.Title
   613.2

ISBN-10 paperback:	1842343181
ISBN-13 paperback:	9781842343180
ISBN-10 hardback:	1842344129
ISBN-13 hardback:	9781842344125

PHOTOGRAPHIC CREDITS
Cover: **The Brown Reference Group plc**: Edward Allwright; **Hemera Photo Objects.**
Title page: **Hemera Photo Objects**
BananaStock: 4, 6, 11, 18, 19, 23, 28; **The Brown Reference Group plc**: Edward Allwright 3, 8, 10, 13, 14, 20, 21, 22, 24, 26, 29, 32; **Corbis**: 17b; **Hemera Photo Objects**: 1, 5, 7, 11,12, 13, 15, 16, 21, 23, 25, 27; **RubberBall**: 9; **Simon Farnhell**: 9, 17,19, 27.

FOR THE EVANS PUBLISHING GROUP

Editor: *Louise John*
Production: *Jenny Mulvanny*
Design: *D. R. ink*
Consultant: *Dr. Julia Dalton BM DCH*

FOR THE BROWN REFERENCE GROUP PLC

Art Editor: **Norma Martin**
Managing Editor: **Bridget Giles**

With thanks to models: **Natalie Allwright, India Celeste Aloysius, Molly and Nene Camara, Abbie Davies, Isabella Farnhell, Georgia Gallant, Heather and Sandy Milligan, Lydia O'Neill, and Sam Thomson**

Important note: *Healthy Kids encourages readers to actively pursue good health for life. All information in* Healthy Kids *is for educational purposes only. For specific and personal medical advice, diagnoses, treatment and exercise and diet advice, consult your doctor.*

Some words are shown in bold, **like this.** You can find out what they mean by looking in the glossary on page 30.

Contents

▶ When you go to bed, you may not feel tired. But soon your eyes shut and you drift off until morning.

Why do we need to sleep?

It looks as if you are doing nothing at all – your eyes are closed and your **muscles** are relaxed. You breathe softly. And you don't see or hear a thing. Your body is relaxing. Your eyes, legs and arms take a break from playing or running around. At the same time, your **brain** is super-active! It files away everything that happened during the day. It helps you understand and remember things. And sleep gives you new energy.

Just amazing!

Sleeping beauty...
● Every week, you spend two to three days asleep. When you are 15 years old, you will have slept for five whole years!

Or try this...

Making sleeping easy...
● Keeping to a regular rhythm is best for your body and mind. Try to go to sleep and get up at the same time every day.

What happens when you sleep?

There are different types of sleep. Each type occurs at a certain stage. In one night's sleep you move through the stages over and over again.

Stage 1 – falling asleep
Your heart beats more slowly and your muscles relax. You may feel as if you are falling. Or your muscles suddenly jerk. Your body temperature drops.

Elephants sleep standing up. They only lie down when they are ready to dream.

Stage 2 – light sleep
You sleep very lightly. It's easy to wake you. Some people talk in their sleep.

Stages 3 and 4 – deep sleep
It becomes much harder to wake you. If you wake up suddenly, you will be confused. Some people walk around during these stages. (Read about that on pages 22–23).

REM-sleep – dreaming
This is when you **dream** all sorts of weird, nice or scary things. (Read more about it on pages 18–21). Everyone dreams each night. But we don't always remember our dreams.

● It's not possible to catch up on sleep you have missed. So, if you don't get enough sleep in the week, you can't 'catch up' at the weekend.

A place to sleep...for a good night's rest

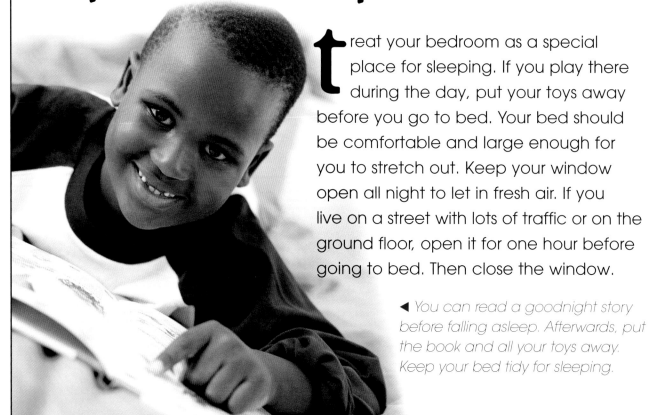

treat your bedroom as a special place for sleeping. If you play there during the day, put your toys away before you go to bed. Your bed should be comfortable and large enough for you to stretch out. Keep your window open all night to let in fresh air. If you live on a street with lots of traffic or on the ground floor, open it for one hour before going to bed. Then close the window.

◄ *You can read a goodnight story before falling asleep. Afterwards, put the book and all your toys away. Keep your bed tidy for sleeping.*

Or try this...

Cutting out lights...
- Use heavy, dark curtains. They hide any bright street lights outside your window and the early morning sunshine.

Cutting out noise...
- Use a quiet alarm clock.
- Switch off fans and buzzing radios.
- Close the windows on a busy street.

How hot or cold?

What temperature?
To sleep well, your bedroom should not be warmer than 20°C.

The room is too hot...
If your bedroom is too hot, you can't sleep. This is why people find it hard to sleep in hot summers.

The room is too cold...
Warm up your bed with a hot water bottle. Remember that you can also wear socks in bed.

▲ *Sharing a bed with your sister, brother or a friend is good fun as long as you both sleep soundly.*

If you're going for a sleepover, pack for hot or cold. Take suitable pyjamas, a sleeping bag and a blanket.

▶ *If you don't like the dark, you can use a night light.*

Or try this...

Sleeping in a tent...
● The tent should have a waterproof base.
● You need a firm inflatable mattress.
● Use a warm sleeping bag, even if it's hot.

7

Getting ready
...before you go to bed

If you go to bed straight after watching an exciting TV programme you can't sleep well. Your mind thinks of everything you saw and did just before bed. It can't calm down. You toss and turn in bed. Prepare your body and your mind so you can go to sleep easily. Follow the same **routine** every day. Always do things in the same order. Then your body and mind know when to fall asleep.

◀ *Have a bath, get into your pyjamas, drink a glass of milk and brush your teeth.*

Do try this...

To help you get ready for bed...
- Eat a light meal early in the evening.
- Do some sports in the late afternoon.
- Drink a glass of milk.

Don't try this...

You can't calm down if...
- You surf the Internet for hours.
- You worry about the next school day.
- You watch upsetting news on TV.

Evening routine

Silly time
Play catch, jog around the garden or tumble about on the floor.

Clearing-up time
Clear away your toys, switch off the TV, video games and computer.

Quiet time
Chill out. Do a jigsaw puzzle, paint a picture or chat with your mum or dad.

◀ *Shout, stretch and run around. Then wind down for bedtime.*

Play a quiet game to settle down before bed. Try colouring or making paper models.

▼ *Read your favourite story or ask an adult to read it to you. You could also listen to a story on tape.*

No chocolates...
● Don't eat chocolate bars or drink fizzy drinks, hot chocolate, coffee or tea. They all contain **caffeine.** It keeps you wide awake.

How to...
Fall asleep

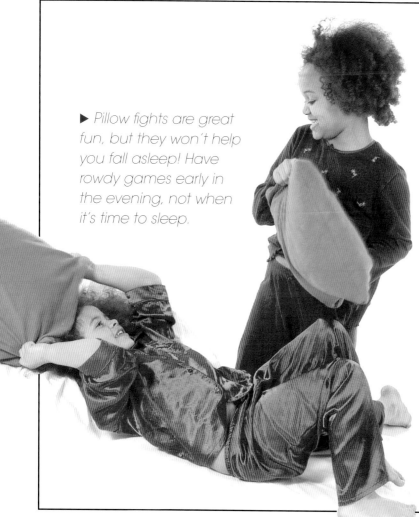

▶ Pillow fights are great fun, but they won't help you fall asleep! Have rowdy games early in the evening, not when it's time to sleep.

Once you are ready, go to bed. It's time to sleep, so stop messing around with your brothers and sisters. Put your book away and switch off your music. If your alarm clock has a light, turn the clock around so you can't see it. Close the curtains. Now turn off the light. Close your eyes and relax. Get ready for a good night's sleep and sweet dreams.

Or try this...

If you really can't fall asleep...
● Discuss it with your parents. Are you going to bed too early? You need 10–12 hours of sleep every night.

● Is someone keeping you awake? A younger brother or sister? Ask your parents if you or they can go to sleep in another room or at another time.

Sleep ideas

read a favourite book

▶ *Brush hair with a soft brush. It feels like a head massage and you'll feel all sleepy.*

listen to quiet music

drink a glass of milk

Don't worry

Write a worry diary

If you worry about things, start a worry diary. Write down what worries you. Now close the diary and put it in the drawer. All the worries are gone for tonight!

Night fright or night light?

A night light helps if you get frightened in the dark. It is dim, but you can see the room.

Just amazing!

Grandpa's bedtime tricks...

Our grandparents used to count sheep to fall asleep: 'one sheep, two sheep...' But counting can keep you awake!

Easy ways to...
Stay asleep

▲ *Wearing socks in bed makes your feet feel warm. It can also be comforting.*

falling asleep is easy, but can you sleep all night through? Some people regularly wake up in the middle of the night. This may happen when a dream is finished. Other people wake up very early in the morning and can't go back to sleep. If this happens to you, try the ideas on page 13. They will relax you. And you can go right back to sleep.

Or try this...

Relax your mind...
Think of your favourite place – a beach or a special place where you went on holiday. Or a park where you play.

Close your eyes. Try to see this place with your eyes closed. Imagine what you can hear.

Relax your body

Loosen up

Lie on your back. Tighten all your muscles. Clench your toes, your feet, your legs, your bottom, your fingers, your hands, your arms, your body, your mouth, your eyes. Stay like that for one minute. Now relax and loosen all the muscles, one at a time. This makes you feel tired and relaxed all over.

Take a deep breath

Lie on your back, with your eyes closed. Take a slow, long, deep breath in. Breathe through your nose, not your mouth. Breathe out slowly and then start again.

The 'teddy' bear was named after Theodore Roosevelt. This U.S. president loved bears and would not shoot them.

▶ *Take a furry toy or snuggle blanket to bed with you. If you wake up, you have something to cuddle up to.*

Or maybe this...

If you have problems sleeping...

- Wear earplugs if you live in a noisy area.
- Lavender relaxes you. Keep some near your bed.
- Learn relaxing **yoga** positions in a class.

13

How much sleep?

how much sleep you need depends on several things. It depends on age. Babies need more sleep than grown-ups. It depends on how active you are during the day. You get more tired if you do lots of sports or hard work. You also need more sleep if you spend a lot of time outside, especially by the seaside. It also depends on what sort of person you are. Some people always sleep a lot.

◀ *If you can't wake up in the morning, you need more sleep.*

Just amazing!

Some animals sleep and sleep...
● Bats are among the sleepiest animals. They spend about 20 hours every day and night in deep slumber.

Others are far too busy...
● The giraffe only sleeps two hours a day.
● The tiny shrew barely closes its eyes for 60 minutes before getting up again.

Changing needs

From baby...

Newborn babies sleep for 16 hours or more every day. They wake up every few hours because they are hungry and need food.

...and child...

When you are five years old, you need about 12 hours of sleep a night. The number of hours you need to sleep gets less as you grow older. An eight year old still needs up to 11 hours of sleep a night. That means going to bed at eight in the evening if you need to get up at seven in the morning! A child aged ten is fine with ten hours.

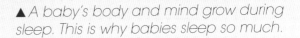
▲ *A baby's body and mind grow during sleep. This is why babies sleep so much.*

...to adult

Adults are happy with seven to eight hours of sleep. Some older people only sleep six hours every night.

Quiz -?-?-?-?-?

1 If you can't sleep, you should...
A ...get up and visit a friend.
B ...think of frightening things.
C ...relax your mind.

2 If you sleep too little...
A ...you won't grow up.
B ...you will feel tired.
C ...you can catch up at school.

ANSWERS: 1C, 2B.

Feeling sleepy?

do you often feel tired during the day? If you yawn a lot or have no energy, you might need more sleep. Your body and brain both need to rest. Your brain can only rest properly if you are asleep. Not being able to sleep is called **insomnia**. It can cause health problems.

▶ *Your brain needs sleep to get its strength back. If you don't sleep enough in the night, you will fall asleep at school!*

Without sleep...

...you get moody

Just frightening...

Dangerous accidents may happen...
● Sleepiness can kill. Many road traffic accidents happen because a car driver did not have enough sleep.

● Some major disasters have happened because someone did not get a proper night's sleep including shipwrecks and at least one large oil spill!

What happens if you don't get enough sleep

If you regularly sleep too little...
...you will get grumpy. If someone makes a joke, you get upset and can't take it. You forget things from one moment to the next. You cannot concentrate. You can't think very well.

When you speak, you sound funny. You slow down and cannot react. You start seeing things that aren't there. You don't think and work well. You may have accidents. Sleep better!

Having too little sleep makes you drop and spill things. You might also bump into furniture and hurt yourself.

...you forget things

...you get very clumsy

Safety first!

Long-term sleeping problems...
● If you have sleeping problems for a long time, go to see your doctor. They will be able to suggest ways to help.

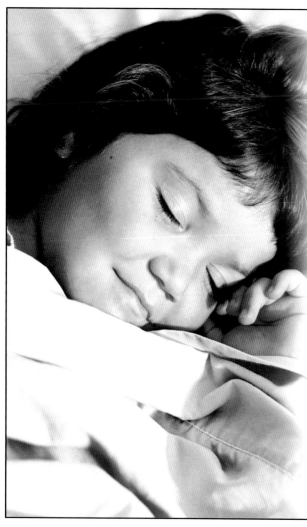

Sweet dreams
Why and what do we dream?

We all dream every night. Sometimes you wake up and remember your dreams. Often you can't remember what you dreamed. You don't dream all night long – there are times with dreams and times without. Your dreams may be like a normal day. Or they can be strange, about **fantasy** figures in exciting faraway lands.

◀ *In your dreams you often see things from your waking day. You might see scenes from TV or people you've met.*

Why is it good for me?

Dreams help you understand life...
- In your dreams, your brain sorts through everything you have done, seen and heard during the day. It 'files' all this information away so you can remember it. It helps you understand events.
- Dreams may also 'exercise' your brain by making new connections in your mind.

Sleep types

There are two types of sleep: **REM** sleep and **non-REM** sleep. Every night, we move from one to the other several times.

REM sleep

REM means 'rapid eye movement'. In REM sleep, your eyes move quickly under your closed eyelids. That is when you dream. Dreams may be very different from your life.

Non-REM sleep

For most of the night we have non-REM sleep. We do not dream much but our body and brain relax and repair themselves.

Dream stories

▶ *Native American dreamcatchers are meant to catch bad dreams and allow only good dreams to get through to you.*

1 *beautiful lands*

2 *dream houses*

Or try this...

Keep a dream diary...

● In the morning, try to remember all you can of your dreams. Write it down and make it into an exciting story.

3 *being able to fly*

Scary dreams
...and being frightened

not all dreams are sweet dreams. Some dreams can be very frightening. Scary dreams are called **nightmares**. Everyone has nightmares from time to time. You may dream of monsters or that you are being chased. You wake up afraid or even screaming – but everything is all right!

◄ *You wake up all of a sudden. Your nightmare seems very real. You're sure there's a monster in your bedroom...*

teeth dropping out

What to do...

When you've had a nightmare...
- Switch the light on so you can see there are no monsters in your room.
- Go to the bathroom. Drink some water.

- If you are very scared, go to see your parents. Tell them about your dream.
- Now go back to bed and to sleep. Try the ideas on pages 10, 11, 12 and 13.

What gives you bad dreams?

Scary stories or films

Horror films are scary. Many other films and stories are also a bit frightening. Even some fairy tales are spooky. You may have bad dreams if you watch scary films or read a frightening book before bedtime.

A frightening world

Adults sometimes talk about things that frighten you. They might talk about losing their jobs or not having any money. The news on TV is also sometimes scary.

If you dream about any of these things, speak to your parents about it.

Family problems

If someone in your family is very ill, you worry about them. If a person you love has died you may have bad dreams. You might have nightmares if your parents are unhappy.

▼ *Having an argument with your best friend can easily make you upset. It might even give you nightmares.*

falling into empty space 1

Or try this...

- Draw a picture of your nightmare.
- Listen to some gentle music.
- Cuddle up to a favourite toy or a soft blanket. Even adults do this!

If you often have scary dreams...

- Tell your parents about it. Talk about what scares you when you are awake and what you dream about at night.

being chased 3

Why do some children...
Walk and talk?

Some children do strange things when they are asleep. They walk around like a robot. Or they talk but don't make much sense. The next day, they can't remember a thing! Sleepwalking and sleep talking are not usually serious problems. They can happen when the person is worried about something. Help them relax to get a good night's sleep.

◀ *Sleeping in a strange room can make some children walk around at night.*

Safety first!

If you share a room with a sleepwalker...
- Make sure all the windows are closed.
- Keep the room free of clutter.
- Clear your toys away before bed.

What is...

...sleepwalking?

Sleepwalkers do strange things in their sleep. They search under the bed, or walk around, or get dressed and take food from the fridge. They look wide awake, but they cannot hear or see you.

...sleep talking?

Some people talk in their sleep. They may answer your questions but often do not make sense.

...snoring?

A blocked nose makes you snore. It gets blocked if you have a cold. If you're still snoring after the cold has gone, see your doctor.

Some sleepwalkers get on a bicycle and ride off. If one child sleep talks, others might join in!

▼ *If you are a sleepwalker, make sure you tidy up before bed.*

- Push chairs under the table.
- Don't leave slippers lying around.
- Do not shout at sleepwalkers or wake them up. Gently lead them back to bed.

Accidents can happen

don't worry if you have an accident and wet your bed. It happens to many children at some point. In fact, one out of ten children aged six wet their beds from time to time. But if it happens often, or even every night, you need to see your doctor. He or she will check if your **urinary tract** is healthy. Stress can be another reason for bedwetting.

◄ Discuss your fears and problems with your mum or dad. Help them remake the bed. They will help you deal with your fears and problems.

Wet facts

it is not your fault 1

Or try this...

If you often wet your bed...

● Do not drink anything just before going to bed. Avoid fizzy drinks, which can make you want to go more often.

● Go to the bathroom several times a day and just before you go to bed. Empty your bladder.

● Do not get ashamed or worried.

What can I do...?

Talk about it

Bedwetting can be a sign that you are worried. If this is true about you, talk to your parents. Perhaps your parents also wet their bed as children. And they can tell you what helped them. If you don't want to talk to your parents, find an adult you trust. You could try talking to an aunt, for example, or to your school nurse. They will be happy to help you.

Alarm bells

Your parents can place a special pad in your bed. It has an alarm bell. The bell rings when the pad gets wet. Your body learns to wake up when you need to go to the toilet. Soon you wake up before the alarm buzzes.

◂▸ The sound of running water can make you want to go to the toilet. Make sure you go before going to bed.

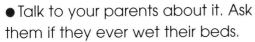

● Talk to your parents about it. Ask them if they ever wet their beds.
● See your doctor to be sure there's nothing wrong with your bladder.

you can learn to stop

you are not alone
2

Waking up
...and feeling fine

mornings can be stressful. But you can easily avoid the early morning rush and family arguments. Prepare as much as you can the night before. Discuss the next day's activities over dinner. Allow enough time for everyone to get ready. If time is tight, get up a little earlier the next day.

◄ *Jump out of bed and have a good stretch. It helps you wake up.*

In the evening...

Get ready for the next day...
● Lay out all the clothes you want to wear the next day.
● Pack your bag for school.

First things first

▲ *Bathe the night before. Then you only need a quick wash in the morning.*

Let the sunshine in

Open the curtains and let light stream into the room. In winter, turn the lights on. It helps you wake up. Some people also like gentle music.

Have breakfast

Don't miss breakfast. After a long night your body needs food. It helps you think better at school.

Clean up and do your tasks

Tidy up. It is nice to come home to a clean and tidy house. Feed the dog or other pets. Have a nice day!

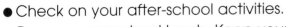

Are you always tired in the morning? Go to bed earlier. Set your alarm a bit earlier to give you time to wake up properly, too.

● Check on your after-school activities.
● Prepare your school lunch. Keep your lunch box in the fridge overnight.
● Set the breakfast table.

Sleeping well for...
A happy life

Sleep well so your body can rest. Do lots of sports, active play and exercises in the daytime. Then you can sleep well at night. A rested body is full of energy. And if your brain gets enough sleeping and dreaming time, you can also think better.

◄ *Smart children get enough sleep so they are wide awake at school.*

calm down before bed

Safety first!

If you can never sleep well...
- Try all the ideas in this book.
- Talk to a parent about your problems.
- Ask your doctor for advice.

See the school nurse or a doctor if...
- You feel stiff or achy most mornings.
- You are more than six years old and often wet the bed in your sleep.

Test yourself

1. Which of these sentences is true?
A A good night's sleep gives you energy for the next day.
B You sleep best in a very hot room, with the windows closed.
C If you can't remember your dreams in the morning, you didn't sleep well.

2. How much sleep do you need?
A About five hours.
B Between ten and 12 hours.
C At least 14 hours.

3. Before going to sleep, you should...
A ...have a large fizzy drink.
B ...drink a glass of milk.
C ...drink and eat nothing for at least five hours before going to bed.

4. To fall asleep easily in the evening, you should...
A ...watch a scary film on TV.
B ...play loud music and have wild and noisy games.
C ...relax and calm down with quiet music and a favourite story.

5. If you have a nightmare, you can sleep better by...
A ...screaming the house down.
B ...taking a deep breath to relax.
C ...telling your parents about it, cuddling up to your teddy bear and thinking of nice things.

ANSWERS: 1A, 2B, 3B, 4C, 5B and C.

follow a routine

• You snore a lot at night, even when you haven't got a cold or flu.
• You always feel sleepy in the daytime.
• You have scary dreams every night.

▶A cold can make you snore. Don't worry – it'll soon go!

relax your body and your mind

Glossary
What does it mean ?

brain *The body part inside your head. It controls what you feel, think and do.*

caffeine *A chemical in cola drinks, tea, coffee and chocolate. It keeps you awake.*

dream *What you imagine, see and feel in your mind while you're asleep.*

fantasy *Something that's not real. But you enjoy thinking or dreaming about it.*

insomnia *When you cannot sleep.*

muscles *Muscles move your bones. You can tense them or relax them.*

nightmares *Very frightening and upsetting dreams.*

non-REM sleep *Several sleep stages when you dream little or nothing.*

REM sleep *REM stands for **r**apid **e**ye **m**ovement. It is the stage of sleep when your eyes move quickly under their closed eyelids. It's also the stage when you dream most.*

routine *Always doing something in the same order, at the same time. It helps your mind and your body relax.*

urinary tract *The parts of your body that make urine and let you urinate.*

yoga *Exercises for body and mind. They help you relax all over.*

To find out more...

...check out these websites
- http://www.sleepfoundation.org/ Website for the National Sleep Foundation.
- www.sleepcouncil.com
- www.sleepdisorders.about.com
- www.coolquiz.com/trivia/explain/docs/sleep.asp

To find out more...

...read these books

● Guber, Tara/Kalish, Leah. *Yoga Pretzels: 50 Fun Yoga Activities for Kids and Grown-ups.* Barefoot Books, 2005.

● Pipe, Jim. *How Long Did I Sleep?* Franklin Watts, 2003.

● Ardley, Bridget. *Oxford Children's A-Z to the Human Body.* Oxford University Press, 2003.

● *Look After Yourself* KS2 CD Rom. Evans Publishing Group, 2006.

● Walker, Richard. *DK Guide to the Human Body.* Dorling Kindersley, 2004.

●www.kidshealth.org/kid/stay_healthy/body/not_tired.html
● www.kidney.org/patients/bw/kidneyboy.cfm
A good explanation of bedwetting.

Index
Which page is it on?